Wounded in
the House of a Friend

Wounded in
the House of a Friend

Sonia Sanchez

Beacon Press
Boston

Beacon Press
25 Beacon Street
Boston, Massachusetts 02108-2892

Beacon Press books
are published under the auspices of
the Unitarian Universalist Association of Congregations.

12 11 10   13 12 11 10

Excerpt from "Angela Davis" by Nicolás Guillén, copyright © 1972
by Robert Marquez and David Arthur McMurray, from *Man-Making
Words: Selected Poems of Nicolás Guillén*, trans., annot., with an
Introduction by Robert Marquez and David Arthur McMurray,
reprinted by permission of the University of Massachusetts Press at
Amherst; excerpt by José Martí, from *Selected Writings of Juan Ramón
Jiménez*, trans. H. R. Hays, copyright © 1957 by Juan Ramón Jiménez
and renewed 1985 by Farrar, Straus & Giroux, Inc., reprinted by
permission of Farrar, Straus & Giroux, Inc.

Text design by John Kane

Library of Congress Cataloging-in-Publication Data

Sanchez, Sonia, 1935–
    Wounded in the house of a friend / Sonia Sanchez.
        p.   cm.
    ISBN 0-8070-6826-8 (cloth)
    ISBN 0-8070-6827-6 (paper)
    1. Afro-American women — Poetry.   I. Title.
PS3569.A468W68   1995
811'.54 — dc20   94-38907

Dedicated with love to

Aliciacita and Roberto
two people who helped me live again

*And one shall say unto
him, What are these wounds in
thine hands? Then he shall
answer, Those with which I
was* wounded in the house of my friends.

Zechariah 13:6

Contents

Part IV *65*

Acknowledgments

Special thanks to the Pew Charitable Trusts of Philadelphia for giving me the time to write and to Temple University for supporting my work.

"Wounded in the House of a Friend" first appeared in *Wild Women Don't Wear No Blues*, ed. Marita Golden, Doubleday, New York, 1993.

"On the Occasion of *Essence*'s Twenty-fifth Anniversary" will appear in a forthcoming book from Essence Communications, Inc., New York, 1995.

"A Love Song for Spelman" first appeared in the *Spelman Messenger*, vol. 105, no. 2, Spelman College, Atlanta, Georgia, 1989.

"Poem" first appeared in *Essence* Magazine, May 1990, Essence Communications, Inc., New York.

"A Remembrance" first appeared in *Essence* Magazine, March 1988, Essence Communications, Inc., New York.

"SweetHoneyInTheRock" first appeared in *We Who Believe in Freedom*, by Bernice Johnson Reagon and Sweet Honey in the Rock, Anchor Books/Doubleday, New York, 1993.

"Bullet Holes of Resistance" first appeared in *Life Notes: Personal Writings by Contemporary Black Women*, ed. Patricia Bell-Scott, W. W. Norton and Company, New York, 1994.

Part I

*I have only one solution: to rise
above this absurd drama that
others have staged around me.*

Frantz Fanon

Wounded in the House of a Friend

Set No. 1

*the unspoken word
is born, i see it in our
eyes dancing*

She hadn't found anything. i had been careful. No lipstick. No matches from a well-known bar. No letters. Cards. Confessing an undying love. Nothing tangible for her to hold onto. But i knew she knew. It had been on her face, in her eyes for the last nine days. It was the way she looked at me sideways from across the restaurant table as she picked at her brown rice sushi. It was the way she paused in profile while inspecting my wolfdreams. It was the way her mouth took a detour from talk. And then as we exited the restaurant she said it quite casually: i know there's another woman. You must tell me about her when we get home.

Yeah. There was another woman. In fact there were three women. In Florida, California, and North Carolina. Places to replace her cool detachment of these last years. No sex for months. Always tired or sick or off to some conference designed to save the world from racism or extinction. If i had jerked off one more time in bed while lying next to her it woulda dropped off. Still i wondered how she knew.

am i dressed right for the smoke?
will it wrinkle if i fall?

    i had first felt something was wrong at the dinner party. His col-
league's house. He was so animated. The first flush of his new job i
thought. He spoke staccato style. Two drinks in each hand. His laughter.
Wild. Hard. Contagious as shrines enveloped the room. He was so wired
that i thought he was going to explode. i didn't know the people there.
They were all lawyers. Even the wives were lawyers. Glib and self-
assured. Discussing cases, and colleagues. Then it happened. A small
hesitation on his part. In answer to a question as to how he would be able
to get some important document from one place to another, he looked at
the host and said: They'll get it to me. Don't worry. And the look passing
back and forth between the men told of collusion and omission. Told of de-
pendence on other women for information and confirmation. Told of nites
i had stretched out next to him and he was soft. Too soft for my open legs.
And i turned my back to him and the nites multiplied out loud. As i drove
home from the party i asked him what was wrong? What was bothering
him? Were we okay? Would we make love tonite? Would we ever make love
again? Did my breath stink? Was i too short? Too tall? Did i talk too
much? Should i wear lipstick? Should i cut my hair? Let it grow? What
did he want for dinner tomorrow nite? Was i driving too fast? Too slow?
What is wrong man? He said i was always exaggerating. Imagining
things. Always looking for trouble.

Do they have children?
one does.

Are they married?
one is.

They're like you then.
yes.

How old are they?
thirty-two, thirty-three, thirty-four.

4

What do they do?
an accountant and two lawyers.

They're like you then.
yes.

Do they make better love than i do?
i'm not answering that.

Where did you meet?
when i traveled on the job.

Did you make love in hotels?
yes.

Did you go out together?
yes.

To bars? To movies? To restaurants?
yes.

Did you make love to them all nite?
yes.

And then got up to do your company work?
yes.

*And you fall asleep on me right after
dinner. After work. After walking the dog.*
yes.

Did you buy them things?
yes.

Did you talk on the phone with them every day?
yes.

*Do you tell them how unhappy you are
with me and the children?*
yes.

*Do you love them? Did you say that you
loved them while making love?*
i'm not answering that.

can i pull my bones
together while skeletons
come out of my head?

i am preparing for him to come home. i have exercised. Soaked in the tub. Scrubbed my body. Oiled myself down. What a beautiful day it's been. Warmer than usual. The cherry blossoms on the drive are blooming prematurely. The hibiscus are giving off a scent around the house. i have gotten drunk off the smell. So delicate. So sweet. So loving. i have been sleeping, no, daydreaming all day. Lounging inside my head. i am walking up this hill. The day is green. All green. Even the sky. i start to run down the hill and i take wing and begin to fly and the currents turn me upside down and i become young again childlike again ready to participate in all children's games.

She's fucking my brains out. I'm so tired i just want to put my head down at my desk. Just for a minute. What is wrong with her? For one whole month she's turned to me every nite. Climbed on top of me. Put my dick inside her and become beautiful. Almost birdlike. She seemed to be flying as she rode me. Arms extended. Moving from side to side. But my God. Every night. She's fucking my brains out. I can hardly see the morning and I'm beginning to hate the nite.

He's coming up the stairs. i've opened the venetian blinds. i love to see the trees outlined against the night air. Such beauty and space. i have oiled myself down for the night. i slept during the day. He's coming up the stairs. i have been waiting for him all day. i am singing a song i learned years ago. It is pretty like this nite. Like his eyes.

i can hardly keep my eyes open. Time to climb out of bed. Make the 7:20 train. My legs and bones hurt. i'm outta condition. Goddamn it. She's turning my way again. She's smiling. Goddamn it.

What a beautiful morning it is. i've been listening to the birds for the last couple hours. How beautifully they sing. Like sacred music. i got up and exercised while he slept. Made a cup of green tea. Oiled my body down. Climbed back into bed and began to kiss him all over . . .

Ted. Man. i'm so tired i can hardly eat this food. But i'd better eat cuz i'm losing weight. You know what man. i can't even get a hard-on when another bitch comes near me. Look at that one there with that see-through skirt on. Nothing. My dick is so limp only she can bring it up. And she does. Every nite. It ain't normal is it for a wife to fuck like she does. Is it man? It ain't normal. Like it ain't normal for a woman you've lived with for twenty years to act like this.

She was killing him. He knew it. As he approached their porch he wondered what it would be tonite. The special dinner. The erotic movie. The whirlpool. The warm oil massage until his body awakened in spite of himself. In spite of an 18 hour day at the office. As he approached the house he hesitated. He had to stay in control tonite. This was getting out of hand.

She waited for him. In the bathroom. She'd be waiting for him when he entered the shower. She'd come in to wash his back. Damn these big walk-in showers. No privacy. No time to wash yourself and dream. She'd come with those hands of hers. Soaking him. On the nipples. Chest. Then she'd travel on down to his thing. He sweet peter jesus. So tired. So forlorn. And she'd begin to tease him. Play with him. Suck him until he rose up like some fucking private first class. Anxious to do battle. And she'd watch him rise until he became Captain Sweet Peter. And she'd climb on him. Close her eyes.

honey. it's too much you know.
What?

all this sex. it's getting so i can't concentrate.
Where?

at the office. at lunch. on the train. on planes.
all i want to do is sleep.
Why?

you know why. every place i go you're there.
standing there. smiling. waiting, touching.
Yes.

in bed. i can't turn over and you're there.
lips open. smiling, all revved up.
Aren't you horny too?

yes. but enough's enough. you're my wife. it's
not normal to fuck as much as you do.
No?

it's not well, nice, to have you talk the way
you talk when we're making love.
No?

can't we go back a little, go back to our
normal life when you just wanted to sleep at
nite and make love every now and then? like me.
No.

what's wrong with you. are you having a nervous
breakdown or something?
No.

*if i become the
other woman will i be
loved like you loved her?*

*And he says i don't laugh. All this he says while he's away in Califor-
nia for one week. But i've been laughing all day. All week. All year. i
know what to do now. i'll go outside and give it away. Since he doesn't
really want me. My love. My body. When we make love his lips swell up.
His legs and arms hurt. He coughs. Drinks water. Develops a strain at
his butt-hole. Yeah. What to do now. Go outside and give it away. Pussy.*

Sweet. Black pussy. For sale. Wholesale pussy. Right here. Sweet black pussy. Hello there Mr. Mailman. What's your name again? Oh yes. Harold. Can i call you Harry? How are you this morning? Would you like some cold water it's so hot out there. You want a doughnut a cookie some cereal some sweet black pussy? Oh God. Man. Don't back away. Don't run down the steps. Oh my God he fell. The mail is all over the sidewalk. hee hee hee. Guess i'd better be more subtle with the next one. hee hee hee. He's still running down the block. Mr. Federal Express Man. Cmon over here. Let me Fed Ex you and anyone else some Sweet Funky Pure Smelling Black Pussy. hee hee hee.

I shall become his collector of small things; become his collector of burps, biceps and smiles; I shall bottle his farts, frowns and creases; I shall gather up his moans, words, outbursts wrap them in blue tissue paper; get to know them; watch them grow in importance; file them in their place in their scheme of things; I shall collect his scraps of food; ferret them among my taste buds; allow each particle to saunter into my cells; all aboard; calling all food particles; cmon board this fucking food express; climb into these sockets golden with brine; I need to taste him again.

you can't keep his dick in your purse

Preparation for the trip to Dallas. Los Angeles. New Orleans. Baltimore. Washington. Hartford. Brownsville. (Orlando. Miami. Late check-in. Rush. Limited liability.) That's why you missed me at the airport. Hotel. Bus stop. Train station. Restaurant. (Late check-in. Rush. Limited liability.) I'm here at the justice in the eighties conference with lawyers and judges and other types advocating abbreviating orchestrating mouthing fucking spilling justice in the bars. Corridors. Bedrooms. Nothing you'd be interested in. (Luggage received damaged. Torn. Broken. Scratched. Dented. Lost.) Preparation for the trip to Chestnut Street. Market Street. Pine Street. Walnut Street. Locust Street. Lombard Street. (Early check-in. Slow and easy liability.) That's why you missed me at the office. At the office. At the office. It's a deposition. I'm deposing an entire office of women and other types needing my deposing. Nothing of interest to you. A lot of questions no answers. Long lunches. Laughter. Penises. Flirtings. Touches. Drinks. Cunts and Coke. Jazz and jacuzzis. *(Morning. Evening. Received. Damaged. Torn. Broken. Dented. Scratched. Lost.)*

I shall become a collector of me.
ishallbecomeacollectorofme.
i Shall become a collector of me.
i shall BECOME a collector of me.
I shall Become A COLLECTOR of me.
I SHALL BECOME A COLLECTOR OF ME.
ISHALLBECOMEACOLLECTOROFME.
AND PUT MEAT ON MY SOUL.

Set. No. 2

i've been keeping company, with the layaway man.
i say, i've been keeping company, with the layaway man.
each time he come by, we do it on the installment plan.

every Friday night, he comes walking up to me do'
i say, every Friday night, he comes walking up to me do'
empty pockets hanging, right on down to the floor

gonna get me a man, who pays for it up front
i say, gonna get me a man, who pays for it up front
cuz when i needs it, can't wait til the middle of next month

i've been keeping company, with the layaway man
i say, i've been keeping company, with the layaway man
each time he come by, we do it on the installment plan
each time he come by, we do it on the installment plan

Part II

I dream of cloisters of marble
when in divine silence,
standing upright, heroes repose:
and at night, in the light of the soul,
I speak to them, in the nighttime!

José Martí

Catch the Fire

For Bill Cosby

(Sometimes I Wonder:

        What to say to you now
        in the soft afternoon air as you
        hold us all in a single death?)

I say—

        Where is your fire?

I say—

        Where is your fire?

        You got to find it and pass it on
        You got to find it and pass it on
        from you to me from me to her from her
        to him from the son to the father from the
        brother to the sister from the daughter to
        the mother from the mother to the child.

Where is your fire? I say where is your fire?
Can't you smell it coming out of our past?
The fire of living . . . . . . Not dying
The fire of loving . . . . . . Not killing
The fire of Blackness . . . Not gangster shadows.

Where is our beautiful fire that gave light
to the world?
The fire of pyramids;
The fire that burned through the holes of
slaveships and made us breathe;
The fire that made guts into chitterlings;
The fire that took rhythms and made jazz;
The fire of sit-ins and marches that made
us jump boundaries and barriers;
The fire that took street talk and sounds
and made righteous imhotep raps.
Where is your fire, the torch of life
full of Nzingha and Nat Turner and Garvey
and Du Bois and Fannie Lou Hamer and
    Martin
and Malcolm and Mandela.

Sister / Sistah. Brother / Brotha. Come / Come.

CATCH YOUR FIRE . . . . DON'T KILL
    HOLD YOUR FIRE . . . . DON'T KILL
    LEARN YOUR FIRE . . . . . . DON'T KILL
    BE THE FIRE . . . . DON'T KILL

Catch the fire and burn with eyes
that see our souls:
                WALKING.
                SINGING.
                BUILDING.
                LAUGHING.
                LEARNING.
                LOVING.
                TEACHING.
                BEING.

Hey. Brother / Brotha. Sister / Sistah.
Here is my hand.
Catch the fire . . . and live.
                    live.
                    livelivelivelive.
                    livelivelivelive.
                    live.
                    live.

On the Occasion of
Essence's
Twenty-fifth Anniversary

I give you my hand in a moment of
sudden love and respect _Essence_ magazine.
You are twenty-five years old, as old as
my twin sons. Having crossed twenty-five
years, I give you my eyes at this hour
of hunger breaking African children into a
fine rain of death;

I give you my heart because you understand
Black women are violets tied in little bunches.
Braids of hurt. The inevitable beat and color.
Whirlwinds of joy and rage. Equalizers of the evening
and morning star. Lovers of the anarchistic tongue.
Mothers in praise of pants and skirts, adjectives
and verbs, chapels and confessionals;

I give you my fist raised against this mad
vibration of death at the end of the twentieth century
where we are filthy with war,
where young veins bleed with lice,

where death cries out like morning birds.
But I have come to you out of Africa out of plantations
out of cities out of suburbs out of colonialism out of racism
out of sexism out of homophobia out of abuse out of alienation
out of my own legs running towards freedom and love
out of time marked by poets;

Now you and I both know as we move
behind the smell of our breathing,
toward the twenty-first century,
that we women must scrub skeletons back to life
exhale our funerals anoint
our feet in light as we genuflect peace and racial justice.
You and I must be reborn in stone in wind in water
kiss life on its two faces
make God finally break the habit of being man.

A Love Song for Spelman

For Dr. Johnnetta B. Cole and Dr. Camille Cosby

1.

What is a love song for Spelman?
Is it a pulse finding us each day at prayer?
If I am to take one voice which shall it be?
A voice stained like iron, dressed for feminine dreams?
What is a love voice for Spelman?
A song walking in tongues, rising and falling like butterflies?

2.

We begin.
With two women seeing the voice of God in the eyes of Black
women.

We begin with newenglandschoolmarms
sisters of silver
creators of light.
Stoking the Southern fires with spit from their White skins.
We begin.

We begin.
With big lips
and dark skins
and woolly hair.
Itinerant eyes in expatriate hearts.
We begin.

We begin.
With a love for freedom
and a thirst for learning.
Tongues heavy with new words
from these our new world lepers.
We begin.

3.

In the long dark basement of shuttered sweat
we sat on benches harder than blue stone.
Some thought us an absurd gathering.
Eleven women of all ages
abundant with mornings.
Hands moving like wings toward knowledge
we came to the basement betrothed to dreams.
And we came to life again.

We came from being not human beings
but hands and feet opening and shutting
in institutionalized work.
We came being not women but trophies
and unremembered bodies hearing our voices in the
delirium of children.

And you told us, O Lord,
that we had to believe that you loved us.
And even though our bodies became stone
we loved you.

4.

We gathered up our skirts, our chins of lard,
from the dark basement to the barracks;
from two teachers to forty-two;
from eleven people to seven hundred;
from one classroom to a campus;
and our breaths agitated rooms and countryside,
became pure and sane and solid and we changed colors
like the seasons and
our hearts burned with fire and
not even the rust of Southern boundaries could stop us.

5.

Like ordained priests: ancient
walking in precise memory.
Like ordained warriors: majestic
Amazon women planting our songs
among the stars and on the waters.
Our songs from farms and cotton fields, from sugar
plantations and slums.
Our songs from urban and suburban roads.
Our songs from Alabama to Georgia, Brazil, and Harlem,
Washington, D.C., and the Congo.
Miracle songs.
Our songs clotting our blood when we bled.
Our songs sweet like eucalyptus against the silence.
Our songs freezing and burning, moving out of corners.
Remaking the air.

6.

Today.
We begin.
A second century of beginnings.
Daughters of great-granddaughters.
Daughters with eyes deeper than flesh.
We begin.
For we are always at the starting point.

We begin
today
with this woman, Johnnetta Cole. A Southern Black
woman.

And we hear her beginning voice
telling us that the dead are never dead.
Their breaths quiver in our shaking hips.
Their voices echo the dew laughing in trees.

We begin
with this woman.

Naming the world as she moves,
"Building for a hundred years hence, not only for today,"
leaving no piece of earth unbaptized.
And we children of all races, daughters from Mozambique
and Soweto, Florida and Mississippi, Cuba and Nicaragua,
outlive our mothers.
And hold our ancestral blood in our hands.

We begin
at this commencement
hearing our foremothers' voices calling to us.
"Listen, Sister Johnnetta. Sister Camille. Spelman
sisters.
Listen: They made me give her up. My last child.
He came and took her and i screamed,
called out to Shango and Damballah and Olukun and Jesus
and Massa to jest let me hold on to her a whilst longer.
Just a few mo days til her eyes got usta seein
without me. But they took her anyways. They took her
whilst i wuz praying on my knees, and i walks slowly now,
my feet rooted to this earth, my footsteps echoin her
brown laughter . . ."

We begin today with these women. Camille Cosby and
Johnnetta B. Cole and all these past and present
Spelman women.
Smelling the evening from under the Sun.

We begin as they twist and turn,
as they call out to our Sister Aunties, Sister Mammies,
Sister Mamas, and tell them that their daughters and
sons dance in our veins. They have heard their
daughters' laughter in the wind.

These two women. These Spelman women. Shaping their
passion, involving themselves in work that brings life
to the middle of our stomachs — call out to our
ancestors to us and our children yet to be born.

Ebe yiye. Ebe yiye. Ebe yiye.° For we have the tools now. We have
the skills and the power. We have the love of self and of our
people to make it better.

Ebe yiye. Ebe yiye. For you Mama dear. For you Mama Sukey
moving in and out of plantation doors. For you Mammy
Teena toiling in the noonday sun. For you young Mama
strutting you big legs down 125th Street in Harlem. For you
Lil Bits. Throat cut in a Chicago alley, for a fix.

Ebe yiye because of our love. Our unity, our strength. Our will.
These two sister women. These Spelman sister women.
Promise you it'll get better for you and me.

Ebe yiye. Ebe yiye. Ebe yiye. Ebeeee yiyeeee.

We begin.

°*It'll get better.*

28

Poem

What I have seen in the twentieth century is the release of Nelson Mandela from 27 years of imprisonment, fist raised in victory, South African spirit still soaring high;

What I have seen in the twentieth century is Malcolm, hurricane man, shaking us free of our wounds, moving us into the fire that cleanses;

What I have seen in the twentieth century is Fannie Lou Hamer, bathing her flesh in freedom, arresting the old South with her vision for a new South;

What I have seen in the twentieth century is Martin, a nonviolent man silenced by violence, sequestering our eyes on mountaintops;

What I have seen in the twentieth century is the wilderness of African-American women, years trembling like butterflies, traversing the limits of pavements and pain, praising our hands in kitchens and corporations in schools and factories in courtrooms and bedrooms, probing for the peace and beauty and power that are ours;

And today. Walking toward the twenty-first century, with our yesterdays feasting on its past, I move as an African woman, disposed to dreams and truth, disposed to cutting through stone while shaping our laughter like rubies.

Today. My simple passion is to write our names in history and walk in the light that is woman.

A Remembrance

The news of his death reached me in Trinidad around midnight. I was lecturing in the country about African-American literature and liberation, longevity and love, commitment and courage. I could not sleep. I got up and walked out of my hotel room into a night filled with stars. And I sat down in the park and talked to him. About the world. About his work. How grateful we all are that he walked on the earth, that he breathed, that he preached, that he came toward us baptizing us with his holy words. And some of us were saved because of him. Harlem man. Genius. Piercing us with his eyes and pen.

How to write of this beautiful big-eyed man who took on the country with his words? How to make anyone understand his beauty in a country that hates Blacks? How to explain his unpublished urgency? I guess I'll say that James Arthur Baldwin came out of Harlem sweating blood, counting kernel by kernel the years spent in storefront churches. I guess I'll say he walked his young steps like my grandfather, counting fatigue at the end of each day. Starved with pain, he left, came back. He questioned and answered in gold. He wept in disbelief at himself and his country and pardoned us all.

When I first read James Baldwin's *Go Tell It on the Mountain* I knew I was home: Saw my sisters and aunts and mothers and grandmothers holding up the children and churches and communities, turning their collective cheeks so that we could survive and be. And they settled down on his pages, some walking disorderly, others dressed in tunics that hid their nakedness. Ladies with no waists. Working double time with the week. Reporting daily to the Lord and their men. Saw his Black males walking sideways under an urban sky, heard their cornbread-and-sweet-potato laughter, tasted their tenement breaths as they shouted at the northern air, shouted at the hunger and bed bugs, shouted out the days with pain, and only the serum of the Lord (or liquor) could silence the anger invading their flesh.

When I first saw him on television in the early sixties, I felt immediately a kinship with this man whose anger and disappointment with America's contradictions transformed his face into a warrior's face, whose tongue transformed our massacres into triumphs. And he left behind a hundred TV deaths: scholars, writers, teachers, and journalists shipwrecked by his revivals and sermons. And the Black audiences watched and shouted amen and felt clean and conscious and chosen.

When I first met him in the late sixties, I was stricken by his smile smiling out at the New York City audience he had just attacked. I was transfixed by his hands and voice battling each other for space as they pierced, caressed, and challenged the crowded auditorium. I rushed toward the stage after the talking was done, I rushed toward the stage to touch his hands, for I knew those hands could heal me, could heal us all because his starting place had been the altar of the Lord. His starting place had been an America that had genuflected over Black bones. Now those bones were rattling discontent and pulling themselves upright in an unrighteous land. And Jimmy Baldwin's mouth, traveling like a fire in the wind, gave us the songs, the marrow and the speech as we began our hesitant, turbulent and insistent walk against surrogates and sheriffs, governors and goons, patriarchs and patriots, missionaries and 'ministrators of the status quo.

I was too shy too scared too much a stutterer to say much of anything to him that night. I managed to say a hello and a few thank-you's as I ran out of the auditorium back to a Riverside

Drive apartment, as I carried his resident spirit through the coming nights, as I began to integrate his fire into my speech. No longer slavery-bound. No longer Negro-bound. No longer ugly or scared. But terrifyingly beautiful as I, we, began to celebrate the sixties and seventies. Opening and shutting with martyrs. A million bodies coming and going. Shaking off old fears. Laughing. Weeping. Hoping. Studying. Trying to make a colony finally into a country. Responsible to all its citizens. I knew finally as the Scriptures know that "the things that have been done in the dark will be known on the housetops."

The last time I saw Jimmy Baldwin was at Cornell University. But it is not of that time that I want to speak, but of the next to the last time we spoke in Atlanta. An Atlanta coming out from under serial murders. An Atlanta that looked on him as an outsider attempting to stir up things better left unsaid.

A magazine editor motioned to me as I entered the hotel lobby at midnight, eyes heading straight for my room, head tired from a day of judging plays. He took me to the table where Jimmy was holding court. Elder statesman. Journeying toward himself. Testifying with his hand and mouth about his meeting with professors and politicians and preachers. He had listened to activists and soothsayers and students for days, and his hands shook from the colors of the night, and the sound of fear fell close to his ears each day.

We parted at five o'clock in the morning. I had seen Atlanta through his eyes, and I knew as he knew that the country had abandoned reason. But he stayed in Atlanta and continued to do his duty to the country. Raising the consciousness of a city. And the world.

I was out of town, traveling in the Midwest on flat lands with no curves, the last time he visited Philadelphia. He had come to speak with poet Gwendolyn Brooks at the Afro-American Historical and Cultural Museum. One of my twins, Mungu, walked up to Jimmy that night, shook his hand and heard his male laughter as he introduced himself. They hugged each other, then my son listened to his Baldwinian talk cast aside the commotion of the night. The next day Mungu greeted me with Jimmy's sounds, and he and his brother Morani thanked me for insisting that they travel to the museum to hear Mr. Baldwin and Ms. Brooks.

SweetHoneyInTheRock

Set 1

What an honor it is for me to write a poem for some downhomeupsouth sweethoneyintherock women, keeping us alive, showing us how to be tough and soft as we walk toward love and liberation;

And i call out to Olukun to part the waters for these women, our sisters who made us look down the corridors of our birth;

What an honor to write a poem for these women who have loved us with their sweethoney breaths.

Set 2

I *Say*
    A Love Poem
                For Sweethoneyintherock

i Say who are these women who
    call themselves sweethoneyintherock;
    who are these sisters strutting on stage
    like Amazons in tambourine laughter,
    Knees dignified with years,
    infinite Knees, not bent on pavements
    corporate teeth or genital grief;
    who are these women singing in glass
    in coal in flames in dust moving us
    from eyes that circumvent God
    from hands that beat women and children into worms;

i Say who are these compañeras
    interrogating our days
    waking us in the flesh alive
    with our grandmother's quilts

with our mother's starched dreams
with our children scouting their birthplace
from our wombs;

i Say. i Say. i Sayyyyyyyy.
who are these women who call themselves
sweethoneyintherock?

Bullet Holes of Resistance

In 1987, I visited Nicaragua with a group of Norteamericano poets. We had come to Nicaragua for the Rubén Darío poetry festival. The festival was held in an outdoor stadium. The sun poured down on our heads. No mercy. But the people entered the stadium with their straw hats. They came to listen to poetry because they loved Darío and other poets. They came. Listened. Nodded their heads in agreement with the message and the beauty. Poetry for people! Poetry for the children! Poetry for the country to live on amid attacks from Contras and other hidden enemies. They clapped and embraced our words as their own. And we were one. For a while. In between bullets and hunger.

Nicaraguan Journal

January 17, 1987 — Saturday nite

Nothing had prepared me for my arrival in Nicaragua. Not my
trip to the People's Republic of China in 1973. Nor Cuba in 1978.
Nothing had prepared me for the emotion i felt as i traveled up
and down those roads, as i counted the bullet holes piercing a
land full of resistance. And our bus hugged the road as if it were
afraid of falling into a great wide hole. (Ah, America. You will
bring them to their knees. Starve them out, huh???) i had come
to this country from other countries. Footsteps walking from un-
der my feet. i had arrived in Nicaragua after many hesitations:
conflict of classes, illness, financial woes, a distance between H.
and me. (i catch him staring into space. Someplace else. He en-
courages our distances i think.) Yet. Here i am / was on this Jan-
uary nite. Inhaling these warm breezes erasing the cold studding
my face. And the nite felt easy. But i heard the city on guard
against earthquakes. Contras. Blackouts. Hunger. Warships off
its Atlantic and Pacific coasts. Hunger. Hunger. Hunger. And
our bus moved toward our *hotelito* humming a sound that re-

sounded with many silences. *La revolución es una chavala de cuatro años*.

MANAGUA. Riding on the bus to our hotel. What one sees in the Caribbean, Central America, how dark it is at nite. And the people, always congregating outside. Just as we did in Harlem. In the summertime, out of the dark, small, dingy houses that tried to restrict, reshape us into shapeless entities.

January 18, 1987 — Sunday

And we came to Ciudad Darío: birthplace of Rubén Darío for the Rubén Darío Poetry Festival. What a day. Hot sun pouring down on our heads. Faces. Loud boisterous sun. With no manners. Doesn't know how to go home. Tomás Borge spoke. i shook hands with him. Told him i had seen him in Cuba in December 1984. Should have requested his autograph. Tom McGrath, Roberto Vargas, Carlos Rygbi read their poetry. And others. All very good! Musicians played. A group from Angola sang and played African instruments. *Muy Bien*. Some of us read in the late afternoon. About 4:45 — read my piece about "we are here for more reasons than history . . ." Carlos translated . . . well received. On the way to Estelí. Near the Honduran border. We walked in the streets. Saw buildings with huge bullet holes. Buildings destroyed by the war. Passed by a disco, loud American music emanating from the creases. The young people came out and looked at us. They were fascinated by Lamont's dreadlocks. They touched them hesitantly.

ESTELÍ. The earth in Estelí sprang up as if seeking me out. i breathed borrowing this Estelí air that has had to heal its own bleeding children and women. i hold out my wounds.

Part III

*Negritude is what one race
brings to the common rendezvous
where all will strive for the
new world of the poet's vision.*

C. L. R. James

Love Song No. 3

1.

i'm crazy bout that chile but she gotta go.
she don't pay me no mind no mo. guess her
mama was right to put her out cuz she
couldn't do nothin wid her. but she been
mine so long. she been my heart so long.
now she breakin it wid her bad habits.
always runnin like a machine out of control;
always lookin like some wild woman trying
to get some place she ain't never been to.
always threatenin me wid her looks.
wid them eyes that don't blink no mo.

i'm crazy bout her though, but she got to go.
her legs walkin with death everyday and
one day she gon cross them right in front of
me and one of us will fall.
here she cum openin the do. comin in wid
him. searchin the room with them eyes that
usta smile rivers, searchin for sumthin to
pick up sumthin to put her 18 years into.

how can i keep welcomin her into my house? how
can i put her out the way her mama did
when she 16 years old and fast as lightnin?
she still got baby fat on her cheeks.
still got that smile that'll charm the drawers
off ya. hee hee hee.

2.

it's gittin cold in here. that's a cold
wind she walkin with. that granbaby of mine.
rummagin the house wid her eyes.
rummagin me wid her look.

where you been to girl? been waitin for you
to come home. huh. how you be walter?
you looking better today girl. marlene
baby we need to talk. we need to sit
down and talk bout what you doin
wid yo life. i ain't gon be here forever. but
this money i give you everyday.
this money you usin to eat up your bones everyday.
this money you need mo of each day is
killin you baby. let me help you outa
this business you done got yo self into.
let me take you to the place miz jefferson
took her son to. you too young and pretty
and smart to just spend yo days walkin
in and out of doors.

yes. i has yo money. yes. i be here when
you come back. but. but. but. alright. Here's
10 dollars. from now on out jest 10 dollars
outa yo mama's insurance money.
that all you need to waste each day on
that stuff. jest 10 dollars. no. i'm not
foolin girl. jest 10 dollars.

3.

what i remember bout her wuz
she was so fat. such a fat baby.
wid smiles. creases. all over her body.
her mama had to work weekends
so she stayed wid me and i sang
and played the radio for her and
the smiles multiplied on her body.
jest one big smile she wuz.
harlem ain't no place to raise a
child though. the streets promise so
much but they full of detours fo
young girls wid smiles on they
bodies. i usta sit on the stoop and
watch her jump doubledutch. her
feet bouncin in and out of that
rope like a ballerinas. i could see
two of her inside that rope she
went so fast. multiplyin herself
on these harlem streets outloud. hee hee hee.
she usta run so fast i couldn't get

these old legs of mine to keep up wid her.
i called out: marlene baby. you jest
remember to stop at the corner. you jest
remember to stop fo you git hit by one
of them cars. you jest remember to stop.

4.

stop it now girl. i ain't studyin you.
stop shovin me. stop it now. you ain't
gittin no mo money. jest the ten dollars.
you got to have sumthin for when you
older. this insurance money your mama
left is you security. yo future.
stop it now girl fo you hurt yoself
help me up offa this floor and put
down that hammer girl. ahahahah.
ahahahahah. don't hit me no mo marlene.
i got to stand up, move
towards her try to touch her wid these
hands that worked in every house in Bklyn
and Longisland to give her them pretty
dresses she usta wear. heeheehee.
i got to try to turn toward her babyfat.
stop it. marlene. AHAHAHAH.
holy jesus. jesus it hurts. holy jesus.
she see me cryin now she gon stop.
she gon remember when i picked her up from her tricycle

and her head wuz bleedin and i run
her to harlem hospital movin like a madwoman
she gon remember how i held
her tears in my dress.
she gon remember how her arms reached out
to me when the doctor gave her them stitches.
i jest gon reach up to her arm with that hammer.
give me you arms again baby. its you granmama.
AHAHAHAHAHAHAHAHAHAHAH
ohmyjesuswhyhasyouforsakenus?
huh? nobodygonrememberherwhenimgone.
theyonlygonseeherwhitebonesstretchedout
againsttheskynobodygonrememberher
younglegsrunningdownlenoxavenuelessenido
marlenebabygivemeyoarms . . . ahahah.
nobody gon remember me . . .

Homegirls on
St. Nicholas

We were the homegirls on St. Nicholas Avenue in Harlem. Grace, Silvia, and I were the good ones who didn't play around or screw the brothers in the gangs. Just casual kisses. Flirtations that led to the front door of an apartment; and nothing else. We were the girls who stood on the stoops and styled our black ballerina shoes and skirts while Bubba and the other brothers looked and laughed and taunted us for our young vanity. And we waited.

We were the homegirls who smiled and danced and kept our dresses down because everybody knew we were going to make something of our lives. And the people on our block waited for their deliverance. The young and the old, the believers and the nonbelievers, waited for us to deliver them from some unspoken curse.

Silvia was the prettiest homegirl on our block. Silvia the singer who looked like Lena Horne. Her voice was small, sparrowlike, but she was beautiful in an angular fashion. Silvia walked her crinoline walk down St. Nicholas Avenue with her long model strides. And we, the shorter ones, followed her strides, imitating her angular pace. Silvia who eloped at 17 and had four babies in four years. Silvia who fell in love with a man as beautiful as she and stopped waiting.

Grace and I went to college. We went our separate homegirl ways. She went South to school, graduated magna cum laude, married a wealthy businessman who carried her off to Europe for their honeymoon. Grace who tripped the light European fantastic each year, a world traveler who wiped her hands on overseas towels and left her footprints behind.

I lived at home during college, walked inside stained-glass Hunter College doors and exited in a four-year flush of females. I borrowed the seasons and fell silent as I set out each day at dawn trying to catch my voice and returned home each night trying to understand my words. The body stayed cold so I packed up my eyes and left.

Where to go when you've been educated not to hear your own echo? Where to go when your soul has lost its beat?

Between sleep and waking I lived. I crowned myself Queen of the Palladium. Remember, O dancers, if you would, the Palladium sitting on Broadway where we mamboed, merengued, and calypsoed till the night fell silent with our rhythms.

It was another of those rallies. New York CORE had planned this rally for weeks. The day was cloudy and grey and wet. As we stood in front of the Hotel Theresa, he ascended the platform. A tall red man. Big Red they used to call him. Now he was Malcolm X. A man I had seen on two other occasions. A man whose eyes made you restless. I turned towards the CORE office. I didn't want to hear him. His words made my head hurt. I was content to picket Woolworth and downtown TV stations. Why did he bring his hand-grenade words into my space?

He stood up and the martial music sounded. I crouched in fear. But I listened on this rainy day and I saw Sundiata and Chaka walking all the way from Africa, spears in their hands. And I saw Bubba running to greet them on our Harlem streets. And the day was like no other.

Malcolm's voice shook the ground. He demanded, "Do you know who you are? Who do you really think you are? Have you looked in a mirror recently brother and sister and seen your Blackness for what it is? Do you know what your Blackness means?"

And something began to stir inside me. Something that I had misplaced a long time ago in the classrooms of America. On that cold wet afternoon, I became warm again. What time of day it was I do not know. What time of year it was I do not remember. All I know is that I began to hear voices — tenants of a long ago past leaped out at me as Malcolm spoke.

And his voice was many voices. And his face became many faces as he spoke. And my skin began to sweat away the years. And the dead skin shook loose and new skin appeared, darker than before. Black in its beauty.

And the day was like no other when he said:

When the people create a program, you get action.

And the years became shorter when he spoke:

We are living in a time when image making has become a science.

They say that Malcolm man don't live here no mo'. They say when a Motswana doctor throws his bones and when they tell him of a loss so terrible he says:

Se iling se ile
Se ile mosimeng, motlhaela-thupa
Lesilo Ke moselatedi. [*]

I say Malcolm lives in the eyes of the homegirls who wait no longer.

[*]*What is gone is gone / It has gone down the hole, the unreachable-by-a-rod / The irrational is he who follows it.*

Introduction of Toni Morrison, and Others, on the Occasion of the Publication of Her Book Race-ing Justice, En-gendering Power: Essays on Anita Hill, Clarence Thomas, and the Construction of Social Reality

Of course it ain't strange that you're here in my
bedroom to accept my nomination of you as Supreme
Court Justice. Barb and I both know how important
bedrooms and beds and bathrooms are to you people . . .
Yes indeedy-by-golly-by-gee. . . . What you say, Barb?
From the outhouse to the White House;

Of course it ain't strange to this journalist that
you will not be on the golf course when you ascend
to that throne of justice. You (and every other Black man)
know the ball's too small;

Of course it ain't strange for the *New York Times*
to delight in your accomplishment of weight lifting.
We all know that Black men's bodies are important
to them, to women, other men, Phil Donahue, academics,
voyeurs, scientists, journalists, oprahwinfrey, undertakers,
prisons, long winding trees;

Of course it ain't strange for this Senator to love your
laugh, to regard it as "second on my list of the most
fundamental points about Clarence Thomas." Yes indeedy-
by-golly-by-gee. . . . Your smile. Your grin. Your loud
laugh. That comes from deep inside and shakes the body
into an American shuffle stirs the soul and I rest
under this proud tradition of your people;

However, it is strange that this dark vindictive-
looking woman could come charging into these hearings
with her accusations — allegations — of
sexual harassment, sexual misdoings,
sexual intimidation. She is evidently put
up to this by those "special interests" people
or she must be crazy or jealous or deranged or
a scorned lover or jealous or a lesbian or insane
or disturbed or a hater of lighter-complexioned women
or jealous. I mean she wasn't raped or nothing
so what's her problem? Where did this college — law
school — educated witch, this ball busting traitor to the
race, this dumb Black female screwing it up
for all Black males trying to succeed, get on with
this sexual harassment stuff? Where she come
from anyway? Who's her mama?

And it is not strange that Mr. Thomas
was not disqualified immediately at the first
charges leveled against him. I mean, we mean,
what does she mean by sexual harrassment, what
does that have to do with work and advancement and
compliance with the rules? After all, doesn't
she know she's Black and female and unmarried
and in need of a job protection advancement verification?
I. We. The men. The country. The world. Have never
heard of a sexually harassed Black woman I don't
care how smart she thinks she is; I mean she's
only a Black woman. Anyone know who's her mama?

Finally it is not strange that we are here with these
"exquisite wordsmiths" who have forged a place for us to

begin to understand the madness of this western psyche,
the madness of men bonding in public against all women.
These writers. These men and women have come to dissect.
Delineate. Decry with brilliance the homicidal nature
of a country that continues to pit Black men and women
in arenas of combat so the executioners can cream
in private with their own pornographic fantasies of how
long and black and how sweetly black it smells.

It is not strange that we have men and women
of conscience here tonite who in defending and
defining Black culture defend the country. The world.
Humanity as well.

So we welcome these wordsmiths. Sister Toni
Morrison. My sister. Sisters Paula Giddings, Nell
Painter, Gayle Pemberton, Kimberlé Crenshaw,
Patricia Williams, Claudia Brodsky Lacour, and
Wahniema Lubiano. And brother Leon
Higginbotham, Jr. My brother. Brothers Cornell
West and Andrew Ross.

And you. My sisters and brothers. This audience
of men/women/students who are here to hear.
Listen.
Listen.
Listen.

Poem for July 4, 1994

For President Václav Havel

1.

It is essential that Summer be grafted to
bones marrow earth clouds blood the
eyes of our ancestors.
It is essential to smell the beginning
words where Washington, Madison, Hamilton,
Adams, Jefferson assembled amid cries of:

> "The people lack information"
> "We grow more and more skeptical"

> "This Constitution is a triple-headed
> monster"
> "Blacks are property"

It is essential to remember how cold the sun
how warm the snow snapping
around the ragged feet of soldiers and slaves.
It is essential to string the sky
with the saliva of Slavs and
Germans and Anglos and French
and Italians and Scandinavians,
and Spaniards and Mexicans and Poles
and Africans and Native Americans.
It is essential that we always repeat:
> we the people,
> we the people,
> we the people.

2.

Let us go into the fields" one
brother told the other brother. And
the sound of exact death
raising tombs across the centuries.
Across the oceans. Across the land.

3.

It is essential that we finally understand:
this is the time for the creative
human being
the human being who decides
to walk upright in a human
fashion in order to save this
earth from extinction.

This is the time for the creative
Man. Woman. Who must decide
that She. He. Can live in peace.
Racial and sexual justice on
this earth.

This is the time for you and me.
African American. Whites. Latinos.
Gays. Asians. Jews. Native
Americans. Lesbians. Muslims.
All of us must finally bury

the elitism of race superiority
the elitism of sexual superiority
the elitism of economic superiority
the elitism of religious superiority.

So we welcome you on the celebration
of 218 years Philadelphia. America.

So we salute you and say:
Come, come, come, move out into this world
nourish your lives with a
spirituality that allows us to respect
each other's birth.
come, come, come, nourish the world where
every 3 days 120,000 children die
of starvation or the effects of starvation;
come, come, come, nourish the world
where we will no longer hear the
screams and cries of women, girls,
and children in Bosnia, El Salvador,
Rwanda . . . AhAhAhAh AHAHAHHHHH

Ma-ma. Dada. Mamacita. Baba.
Mama. Papa. Momma. Poppi.
The soldiers are marching in the streets
near the hospital but the nurses say
we are safe and the soldiers are
laughing marching firing calling
out to us i don't want to die i
am only 9 yrs old, i am only 10 yrs old
i am only 11 yrs old and i cannot
get out of the bed because they have cut
off one of my legs and i hear the soldiers
coming toward our rooms and i hear
the screams and the children are
running out of the room i can't get out
of the bed i don't want to die Don't
let me die Rwanda. America. United
Nations. Don't let me die . . . .

And if we nourish ourselves, our communities
our countries and say

        no more hiroshima
        no more auschwitz
        no more wounded knee
        no more middle passage
        no more slavery
        no more Bosnia
        no more Rwanda

No more intoxicating ideas of
racial superiority
as we walk toward abundance
we will never forget

        the earth
        the sea
        the children
        the people

For *we the people* will always be arriving
a ceremony of thunder
waking up the earth
opening our eyes to human
monuments.
    And it'll get better
    it'll get better
if *we the people* work, organize, resist,
come together for peace, racial, social
and sexual justice
    it'll get better
    it'll get better.

This Is Not a Small Voice

This is not a small voice
you hear   this is a large
voice coming out of these cities.
This is the voice of LaTanya.
Kadesha. Shaniqua. This
is the voice of Antoine.
Darryl. Shaquille.
Running over waters
navigating the hallways
of our schools spilling out
on the corners of our cities and
no epitaphs spill out of their river mouths.

This is not a small love
you hear   this is a large
love, a passion for kissing learning
on its face.
This is a love that crowns the feet with hands
that nourishes, conceives, feels the water sails
mends the children,

folds them inside our history where they
toast more than the flesh
where they suck the bones of the alphabet
and spit out closed vowels.
This is a love colored with iron and lace.
This is a love initialed Black Genius.

This is not a small voice
you hear.

Part IV

I have come to tell you you are beautiful.
I believe you are beautiful,
But that is not the issue.
The issue is they want you dead.

Nicolás Guillén

Like

Like

All i did was
go down on him
in the middle of
the dance floor
cuz he is a movie
star he is a blk/
man "live" rt off
the screen fulfilling
my wildest dreams.

Like.

Yeah. All i did
was suck him in tune
to *that's the way love goes*
while boogeying feet
stunning thighs pressed
together in rhythm cuz he

wanted it and i wanted
to be seen with him
cuz he's in the movies on the
big screen bigger than life
bigger than all of my
hollywood dreams
cuz see
i need to have my say
among all the unsaid
lives i deal with.

Like.
Yeah.

Eyewitness:
Case No. 3456

i was raped at 3 o'clock one morning. i was sleeping in my bedroom in the back part of my house. And i awakened with a hand on my mouth and a knife at my throat. i tried to scream but the screams choked on his hand. He started to talk. Said he would kill me if i screamed. Began to move the knife across my body, making little nicks. Said he could make me less a woman if he cut off my breasts and i began to pray called on my Gods to help me survive the night and he scraped my skin with the knife, as if he was trying to remove the color from me.

Don't you look at me he screamed as he moved the knife toward my vagina. Don't you open yo mouth or yo eyes or you dead. Bitch. Bitch. Yeh. Bitch. Bitch. Blk mothafucking bitch.

And then he tore off my gown and pushed my legs up and went inside me. He was soft. i thought, this won't hurt too much. Then he screamed, *move yo ass* bitch cmon move yo ass with me you know you want this yeah that's it move yo ass i'm gon give you a fuck like you ain't never had and as he talked he got harder and harder and he jabbed his penis from one side to another up against my fibroids and i screamed and he socked me, said, start talking bitch say it's good it feels good tell me how juicy it is tell me how you love the pain go on talk to me bout big black dicks and sucking big black dicks yeh here i come with mine cmon suck me off cmon lick him suck him feel my balls. . . . Ahhhh yes yesss. Smile bitch this here's mo fucking you've had in a long time. Go on suck him hard that's it oh that's it keep him hard cuz he gon rip you up inside. Turn over yeh turn over i want to see what you got back there.

And i screamed O my God no don't. Don't. And he hit me in the head pushed my mouth flat down on the bed. i cdn't breathe. i thought i would suffocate then and there and he pulled my head up and whispered in my ear don't mess with me bitch. Push yo ass up and enjoy. . . . Ahhhh. And the pain flooded through me like saltwater. And the pain stretched from my anus to my throat and he said move your ass baby that's it move yo ass huh you really tight there you aint never been fucked in the ass befo. So i'm the first i'm the first. hey hey hey. im coming. im coming now cmon giddy up giddy up there bitch move yo ass move yo ass groan bitch moan bitch tell me you love this you want this you need this. Stop crying or i'll kill yo ass cmon say it now. . . .

This is. . . . This is. . . . This is the best. . . . This is the best fuckin ever man. Fuck. Cmon man do it do it do it yes. That's it feels good oh it feel so good. Fuck me. Fuck me, fuck me hard, fuck me, fuck me. . . . Oh my God, Oh my God. . . .

That's it bitch keep on ooowe ooowe here i come ready or not here i come ooowee oooowe oooowee

When i awoke in the morning he was gone. i dragged myself out of the bed and looked under beds, inside closets under beds, inside other rooms, under beds, ran out of the house, to the porch, and felt the blood on my legs held the blood in my hand saw that the morning had returned and put on my face.

Poem for Some Women

huh?
   i'm all right
   i say i'm
   all right
what you lookin at?
   i say i'm all right
   doing ok
   i'm i'm i'm still
   writin producin on the radio
   who i fooling
   i'm a little ill now
   just got a little jones
     jones jones jones
     habit habit habit

   took my 7 yr old to
   the crack house with me
   on Thursday
   beautiful girl.
   prettiest little girl

her momma done ever seen
took her so she understand
why i'm late sometimes with
her breakfast dinner bedtime
meetings bedtime love.
Wanted her to know how
hard it is for me you
know a single woman
out here on her own you know
and so i took her to the
crack house where this
man. This dog this
former friend of mine lived
wdn't give me no crack
no action. Even when
i opened my thighs to give him some
him again for the umpteenth
time he sd no all
the while looking at
my baby my pretty
little baby. And he
said i want her. i need
a virgin. Your pussy's
too loose you had
so much traffic up
yo pussy you could
park a truck up there
and still have room
for something else.
And he laughed this long laugh.
And i looked at him and the
stuff he wuz holding in his
hand and you know i cdn't
remember my baby's
name he held the stuff out
to me and i cdn't remember
her birthdate i cdn't remember
my daughter's face. And
i cried as i walked out that door.

What's her name, puddintang
ask me again and i'll tell
you the same thing
cdn't even hear her
screaming my name as he
tore into her pretty little
panties
　　"prettiest little girl
　　you ever done seen
　　prettiest little mama's
　　baby you done ever seen."

Bought my baby this pretty
little leather jacket off the street
when i went to pick her up Sunday
7 days later i walked right
up to the house opened the
door and saw her sitting
on the floor she sd Momma
where you been? Momma i
called for you all week
Momma Momma Momma they
hurt me something bad i
want to go home. Momma.

Momma's little baby
loves shortening shortening
Momma's little baby
loves shortening bread
put on the jacket
put on the jacket
Momma's little baby
loves shortening bread

When we got home she
wdn't talk to me. She just
sat and stared. Wdn't watch
the t.v. when i turned it on.
When we got home she just

stared at me with her eyes
dog like. Just sat and
looked at me with her eyes til
i had to get outa there
you know.

My baby ran away
from home last week my sweet
little shortening bread ran
away from home last nite and
i dreamed she was dead
i dreamed she was
surrounded by panthers who
tossed her back and forth nibbling
and biting and tearing her up. My little
shortening bread ran away last week
peekaboo i see you and
you and you and you
and you.

Improvisation

At the Painted Bride with Khan Jamal

Ha ha.
ooooooooooo ai yi yi yi yi yi yi
hee hee hee
hee hee hee hee hee hee hee hee hee
I I'm
I I'm, I I'm I I'm I I'm I I'm I I'm
IIIIIIIIIII am
Hee Hee hee hee hee hee hee hee hee hee hee ah

I was I am
I was I am
I am I was
I am I was I am
I ammmmmmmm
a ha ha ha
It was
It was the coming
It was the coming that was bad
It was it was it was the coming across the ocean that was bad
It was the coming

It was the coming that was bad
It was it was it was the packing
the packing the packing the packing
the packing of all of us in ships that was bad
it was the packing
it was the packing
it was the packing of all of us in ships that was bad
it was the coming
it was the coming
it was the crossing
it was the crossing
it was the crossing
it was the crossing
it was the crossing
it was the crossing that was bad

it wassssssssssssssssssssssssss
the raping that was bad
it was the raping that was bad
it was the raping
it was the raping
it was the raping that was bad
it was the the the the the the the the silence
the the the the the the noise
the the the the the the the silence
the the the the the the noise
the the the the the the silence
the the the the the the noise
the the the the the the the silence
the the the the noise
the the the the silence
the the the the noise
the the the the silence
the noise the noise
the silence the silence
the noise the noise
the silence

it wasssssssssssssssssssssssssssssss
ha ha ha

I am I am I am I am I am I am I am I am
I was I was I was I was I was I was I was
It It It It
It was the boat
It was the boat
It was the boat
It was the ship
It was the ship
It was the landing that was bad
It was the landing that was bad
It was the landing that was bad
It was It was It was
It was the standing on
It was the standing on auction blocks that was bad
It was the standing on auction blocks blocks blocks blocks
Don't don't don't don't don't don't don't don't
don't don't touch me
don't don't don't don't touch me
don't don't don't don't touch me
don't don't don't don't don't don't don't touch me
please please please please please
ah ah ah ah ah ah ah ah ah ahhhhhhhhhhh
ahhhhhhhhh Olukun   Ayo   Olukun
It was the standing standing standing that was bad
It was It was It was It was
It was the giving birth that was bad
It was the giving birth that was bad
Every nine months, every nine months
Every nine months, every nine months
Every nine months, every nine months
ah ah ah ah ahhhhhhhhh
I am I am I am I am I am I am I am
I was I was I was
I shall be I shall be
I am I am
I was I shall be I was I am
I was I am
I was I am
I was I am am am am
oh oh oh oh oh oh

Mother Mother Mother Mother Mother Mother
Father Father Father Father
They know not what they do here
do there do there do there do there
You want to know who I am huh?
want to know who I am huh?
Huh? Huh?
Can't you see who I am un huh
Can't you see who I am huh
Don't you know who I am
Can't you see who I am
I ammmmmmmmmmmmm
ah ah ah ah
I ammmmmmmmm am am am am am
ammmmmmmmmmmmmmm

What what what what what what
Where where where where are you?
Where are you?
Where
What
There you are!
There you are!
There you are!
There you are!
Thought I lost you
There you are!
There you are!
Looking at me eee
Looking at me eee
Looking at me eee
Looking at me eee ah
Looking at me
I'm not looking at you ou
I'm not looking at you
You're looking at me
Looking at me
Looking at me
Looking at me

Looking at me
Looking at meeeeeeeeee

Whatever
I remember I forget
Whatever I forget I remember
Whatever I don't want to remember I forget
Whatever I want to forget I remember
I remember
I remember
I remember
I remember
I remember
I am here
They're here
They're here
They're here
They're here
I am here here here here
Love love love
love love love
love love love
love love love
What is it
love love love
You don't know
know know know
You know we know
you know we knowwwwwwwwwwwwwww

It was
the coming that was baddddddddddddddd
It was the coming that was baddddddddddddd
across oceans across seas across eyes staring
It was the coming coming coming coming coming
coming dying living dying living coming dying living
living dying coming coming dying living
living ing ing

How to live.
How to live.
How to live . . .
How to live . . .
How to live . . .
How to live . . .

blues haiku 1

all this talk bout love
girl, where you been all your life?
ain't no man can love.

tanka

i have taken five
baths ten showers six shampoos
and still i smell her
scent oozing from the quiet
peeling of our lives.

haiku 4

your breath in exile
from me waiting to escape
my persistent air.

haiku 6

if i had known then
what i know now, i would have
picked my own cotton.

South African tanka

the necklace i bring
you is a different one my
love it burns our
history in your flesh it
smells behind the ear of God.

haïku 8

i am hunched down in
veins of fur thick arrows plump
with my depression.

blues haiku 2

ain't no curves in his
talk girl can't trust a man with
no curves on his tongue.

*I do battle for the creation
of a human world — that is,
a world of reciprocal recognition.*

Frantz Fanon